IMAGES
of America

REHOBOTH, SWANSEA, AND DIGHTON

About the Authors

Charles Turek Robinson, a freelance writer, is the author of four books on New England history and folklore, including two regional best-sellers. His articles have appeared in *Yankee*, *The Providence Journal-Bulletin*, *The Journal of the Rhode Island Medical Society*, and numerous other regional, national, and international publications.

Frank DeMattos, head curator of The Carpenter Museum, is president of the Anawan Historical Society, a member of the Rehoboth Antiquarian Society, and an elected member of the Rehoboth Historical Commission. He is co-author of *Rehoboth Through The Ages*.

Contents

Acknowledgments 6
Introduction 7

Rehoboth
1. Tending the Till 9
2. Having Some Fun 21
3. Tilling the Soil 29
4. Teaching Our Tots, Tending Our Souls 37
5. Turning Back the Clock 43

Swansea
1. The Clank of the Coin 53
2. Laughter and Leisure 63
3. People of Prominence 69
4. The Pastoral Past 73
5. Moving About 77
6. Keeping Our Faith, Expanding Our Knowledge 83
7. Going to the Grove 89

Dighton
1. Trade and Industry 93
2. Fun and Frolic 101
3. Plow and Pasture 109
4. Bibles and Books 115
5. Mount Hope Memories 123

Acknowledgments

The authors deeply appreciate the assistance of the following persons and organizations:

The Swansea Historical Society; Helen Pierce; Elaine Varley; the Swansea Public Library; the Dighton Historical Society; Joan Horton Olson; the Carpenter Museum; Joseph Carpenter; the Bristol County Agricultural School; James DeMelo; Dorothy Oliveira; the Horbine School Association; Alfred Rubio; Otis Dyer; Kevin Lawton; Elgin Boyce; Abby Aldrich Hoge Casplar; the Rehoboth Antiquarian Society; Elizabeth Viall; Joel Kinne; Rita Hunter; Theresa Pike; Jeanette Vincent; George Grenon; Mrs. Gilbert DeMattos; Otis Dyer Jr.; Frederick Morth; Miss Hilda Mederios; and Jamie Carter of Arcadia Publishing.

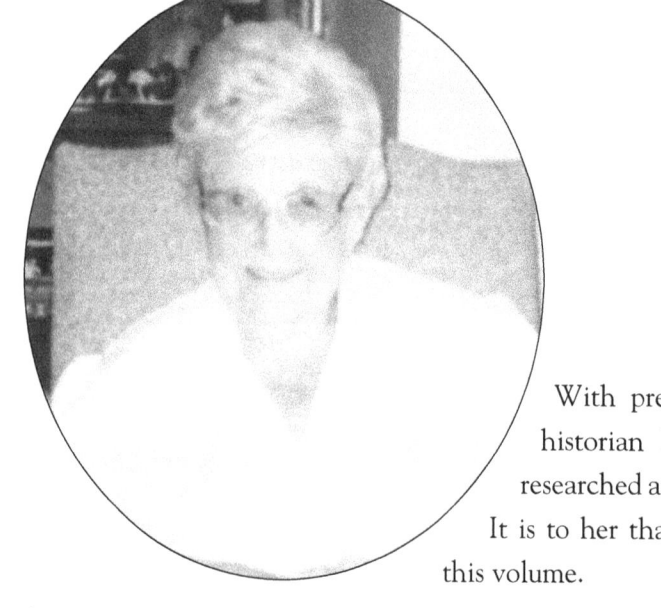

With precision and passion, Swansea historian Helen Pierce has studiously researched and documented the area's past. It is to her that the authors fondly dedicate this volume.

Introduction

by Charles Turek Robinson

There is perhaps no better way to experience and savor the past than through old photographs. Certainly, historical treatises and texts are critical tools for the historian, but the printed word alone cannot fully capture the flavor, texture, and essence of past events, places, and people. Supplemented with historic photographs, the study of history becomes a living, animated process in which the past is visualized and experienced in a manner no amount of reading can duplicate.

Long ago, the towns of Rehoboth, Swansea, and Dighton were more intimate places than they are today. In its visual approach, this book provides a bridge back to that long-gone, quieter, and gentler rural past. By *showing* people and places as they actually appeared, my co-author and I seek to offer human details and textured specifics over abstract historical generalizations. In other words, our primary aim is to bring the area's past—just for a moment—back to life.

This book represents a comprehensive offering of rare historical photographs—derived from various library, school, and historical society archives—that have heretofore gone unseen by the general public and, in many cases, even by area historians. Most of the photographs date from between 1850 and 1950, a century that saw significant changes in Rehoboth, Swansea, and Dighton. While my co-author and I hope to provide a visual record of the area's general transformation from the primarily agricultural setting of previous times to the more suburban-like, residential setting of today, it is not our intent to offer a chronological, sequential, complete history of each town from its founding. Obviously, each township was established many years before the advent of photography, thereby rendering a complete, comprehensive photographic overview impossible. Additionally, many important town events and people were never photographed (and even if they were, space limitation would not allow for inclusion of all of them).

Rather, our book seeks to provide glimpses—some of them breathtaking—of what life was like in nineteenth and early-twentieth-century Rehoboth,

Swansea, and Dighton, and to convey in images the intimacy of small-town life that preceded the progressive impersonalization of more recent times. Via the photo captions, the book also presents a variety of interesting historical facts which, while not aiming to present a complete, chronologically sequential area history, do represent an array of lesser-known, interesting historical tidbits about nineteenth and early-twentieth-century life in the area. One of the book's photographic captions, for instance, describes the little-known Rehoboth house of famous news anchor Walter Cronkite's great grandmother.

Those academically minded individuals who seek complete, historical overviews of Rehoboth, Swansea, and Dighton are referred to the fine, comprehensive works of historians like Bowen, Tilton, and Bliss. Our book is meant not so much for the academic historian but rather for the time traveler who would like to step fifty or a hundred or a hundred and fifty years into the past in order to *visually* glimpse even the simplest of bygone human moments and meanings.

Charles Turek Robinson
Rehoboth, Massachusetts
October 6, 1997

Rehoboth: Chapter One

Tending the Till

The Orleans Manufacturing Company, now an overgrown, skeletal stone ruin on Reed Street, was, when it looked like this in the mid-nineteenth century, a thriving textile mill owned by Benjamin Peck and several partners. Here, many Rehoboth women and children spent their days spinning cotton (from New Orleans, hence the name) into yarn and cloth. The stone building shown here was not the original, having been built in 1831 after an earlier building burned down. In 1884, the mill again burned down and never resumed business.

Known as the Forge Privilege, this building, located on Pond Lily Avenue, housed an iron forge started in 1765 by Ebenezer Peck and sons. The forge was an important supplier of raw iron to Rehoboth-area blacksmiths. Long after it went out of business, the mill stood for many years and became Rehoboth's last mill building until it was, sadly, burned down in the 1960s by an owner wanting to clear the property.

These people, pictured in 1878, worked at the Perry Turning Mill in the Perryville section of town. Started in 1831 by Daniel Perry, the mill made, among other things, butter molds, rolling pins, tools, and tool handles. The turning mill was purchased from Daniel by his brother Charles in 1871, after which it evolved into a sawmill and later a gristmill. The building occupied the site until the late 1930s.

The John C. Marvel general store in Rehoboth Village, pictured here about 1890, was also the town's post office until it burned down in 1899, along with John's adjacent residence. It was in stores like this one—in the days before suburban malls and department stores—that the local rural populace had its primary (and often only) access to a wide variety of diverse goods.

John Cotton Marvel converses with a customer behind the counter of his general store and post office (pictured above). Notice the many diverse goods behind the proprietor, from groceries to cloth to shoes—even to opium-laced paregoric for the childrens' teeth (among other uses). The photograph dates from c. 1893.

Founded in 1809, the Rehoboth Union Manufacturing Company (center) stood directly opposite the village waterfall in Rehoboth Village. The company, which manufactured cotton yarn, was the largest building in the village at the time. Purchased from its original owners by Nelson and Darius Goff in 1829, the company was eventually moved to Pawtucket in 1846 and still operates today as the Union Wadding Company. The original Rehoboth village building was demolished in 1898 to make way for the trolley line.

Folsom's blacksmith shop once stood as a very popular business in the Rehoboth Village from the nineteenth century well into the 1930s, when business finally began to wane. (The new forms of technology that emerged from World War II allowed farmers in Rehoboth and elsewhere to begin to increasingly work with horseless machinery—like the tractor—thereby rendering blacksmith shops like this one somewhat obsolete.)

Kingman's Country Store, pictured here about the turn of the century, was located at the corner of Chestnut and Brook Streets. It was operated by Hiram Kingman, and before that by Edward Horton. Upon Hiram's death in 1910, the store closed its doors. The building is now a private residence.

Rehoboth farmer George W. Holden stands in a long white coat in 1890 on Providence's Pine Street. He is likely procuring—for transport back to his Rehoboth farm—certain non-rural provisions available at that time only in the larger surrounding cities. To the left of George is one of his favorite horses, Dolly; his traveling companion, Spot the dog, stands to the right.

The Willie Goff General Store, located on the corner of Perryville Road and Anawan Street, opened in 1901. In this 1910 photograph, Will Goff and George Munroe chat in front of the store, while Will's children Ruth and Earl sit on the lawn to left. In 1935, the business ceased operations as a general store and became a welfare station (a facility for distributing free food to the needy) during the Depression. The store building is presently a private residence.

F.H. Horton's store is shown here in 1918. Because of its central location in Rehoboth Village, Horton's was—compared to the area's other, more remote general stores—perhaps the most accessible and busiest commercial establishment in town. It closed in 1952, about the time the old general grocery and variety stores were giving way to the modern "supermarket."

The Old Rehoboth Post Office in Rehoboth Village is shown here in 1924, prior to many additions and renovations. It was finally closed in 1984 and replaced by the town's present post office. Standing in front is Edward Earle. At this time, the post office was also a general store, like the earlier John C. Marvel store that had burned to the ground in 1899. Interestingly, in 1927, a twister passing through town ripped the building 6 feet off its foundation.

Joseph Vincent's grocery store, located on Brook Street and pictured here c. 1910, was, interestingly, also a popular dance hall. In 1920, Joseph's eight sons converted the store into a shoe factory that thrived (producing as many as 5,500 pairs a week) for many years. Finally, due to foreign competition, the company (known as the A.L. Vincent Shoe Company) closed in 1938. The building was subsequently occupied by Rousseau and Petit Bodyworks for many years.

Shady Bend, on the banks of the Rehoboth Village pond, served many purposes from the early nineteenth century on. The small building was first an office for the Rehoboth Union Manufacturing Company and served many years later as a combined grocery store and temporary post office. Opened as a tea room by Annie Gilman in the early 1920s, it became a popular eatery until the tea room was eventually closed and replaced by a barber shop (operated for many years by Oscar Berghman). The building has since served as a private residence.

SHADY BEND
Tea Shop
Rehoboth, Mass

Sliced Ham, Egg Salad, Muffin	.50
Sliced Ham, Potato Salad, Muffin	.50
Fried Ham and Eggs, Muffin	.50
Egg Salad	.35
Potato Salad	.25

Sandwiches

Chicken Salad and Tomato	.25
Fried Ham and Egg	.25
Chicken Salad	.20
Fried Ham	.20
Toasted Cheese	.15
Sliced Ham	.15
Tomato and Lettuce Salad	.15
Egg Salad and Olive	.15
Ground Ham and Nut	.15
Cream Cheese and Olive	.10
" " " Nut	.10
Ground Ham	.10
Egg Salad	.10
Lettuce Salad	.10
Sliced Cheese	.10
Marmalade	.10
Jelly and Nut	.10
Jelly	.05
Peanut Butter	.05
Buttered Toast	.10
" " + Marmalade	.25

Desserts

Home-made Pie	.10
Home-made Cake	.10
Apple Pie and Ice Cream	.15
Ice Cream	.10 & .15
College Ices	.20

Strawberry Cherry Raspberry
Pineapple Maple Walnut Fudge

Foams	.15

Strawberry Orange
Raspberry Ginger

Sundaes

Banana Royal	.20
Banana Split	.25
Sweet Sixteen	.25
Fudge Nut	.25
Cherry Walnut	.25
Rehoboth Beauty	.30

Drinks

Hot Tea	.10	Hot Coffe	.10
Iced Tea	.10	Iced Coffe	.10
Milk	.05	Moxie	.10
Orange Ade	.08	Ginger Ale	.08
Sarsaperilla	.08	Birch Beer	.08
Root Beer	.08	Raspberry	.08
Lemon and Lime	.08	Strawberry	.08

Old tea room menu 1922-24

This menu for Annie Gilman's tea room dates from c. 1922–24.

In 1931, Joseph W. Dias opened a Ford car and truck dealership on Rt. 44 (present site of Bradley Oil Company). Joseph was an astute businessman, and the business thrived despite the Depression. After temporarily closing during the war years, the business reopened in 1945 as a Chrysler dealership and remained in business until 1959.

The Hi-Way Market on Rt. 44, Rehoboth's first "modern" supermarket (though small and primitive by today's standards), was opened in 1947 by Manuel DeMattos. This new concept in grocery shopping was—in Rehoboth as elsewhere—quite a dramatic departure from the very personalized mercantile ways of old. Instead of buying over the counter from an attendant, shoppers cruised the store on their own, picking out goods for themselves without assistance and placing them into shopping carts.

In a sense, this early composite photograph of what is now the intersection of Routes 44 and 118 keenly reflects the great physical changes that can be rendered by commercial developers—in a very short space of time—in rural towns like Rehoboth. The Anawan Inn (left) had, throughout the nineteenth century and into the early twentieth, variously served over the years as a stagecoach stop, a tavern, a hotel, an illegal gambling den, a farm, and, finally, a bar. Its colorful and textured history spanning more than a century was, within a mere day in 1971,

razed to the ground, to be replaced shortly thereafter by the current Mobil gas station. Further adding to the rapid and dramatic commercial transformation of this historic town center was, within a short space of ten years, the demolition of surrounding historic structures (for instance, the Rehoboth Garage was replaced by a present-day Cumberland Farms, and a historic stable—to the far right in the above photograph—was replaced by a present-day Dunkin Donuts).

Pictured here, c. 1940, is the second Viall's Ice Cream Parlor to stand on this particular Route 44 site (the first, built just a few years previously, burned down in 1938). Many locals still recall the thrill of their 10¢ ice cream cone. The later advent of larger chains like Howard Johnson's was one reason (among others) for the demise of smaller Route 44 businesses like this one.

"Pop's Red Lantern," pictured here c. 1949 at the corner of Routes 118 and 44, was where Rehoboth residents could get ice cream, penny candy, and, most importantly, the latest in choice town gossip. In the mid-1950s, the store's popular proprietor, "Pop" Alburn, sold the business (which was then renamed the Mid-way, because it stood mid-way between Providence and Taunton). Today, the building serves as the office of realtor David Smith.

Rehoboth: Chapter Two

Having Some Fun

A renowned annual tradition that attracted some 1,800 people (once even including Calvin Coolidge) at its peak in the early part of the century, the Rehoboth Antiquarian Society Clambake commenced in 1886. Pictured here in 1909, the once well-attended event gradually diminished in popularity during World War II and was finally discontinued in 1957. While it has never again become the crucial Rehoboth social event that it once was, the annual clambake resumed in 1984 and has continued to the present day at its traditional Goff Memorial Hall site.

The first Anawan Grange clambake was held *c.* 1908 at Grange Hall (formerly the Anawan Union Baptist church). Note the church steeple, which is no longer on the building.

This photograph of heavy traffic and parking on Route 118 recalls the large turnout for the premiere Grange clambake described above.

This town clambake, c. 1910, was held at the Colonial-era home (in the background) of George Nichols. It was the former Colonel Thomas Carpenter home and the most elaborate Rehoboth house of Colonial times.

This poster advertises the 1903 Antiquarian Society Clambake.

Manuel DeMattos, during a c. 1925 snowstorm, leads a horse cart carrying, from left to right, Al Rubio, Carlos Rubio, and Tony DeMattos. This photograph was taken at the sharp right-angle corner on Summer Street just below the DeMattos Farm.

The Rehoboth team of the Inter-Church Basket Ball League is shown here in a 1930 newspaper photograph—the year they won the league championship. From left to right are as follows: (front row) Carl Berghman, Howard Croome, Fred Bowen, and John Catlow; (middle row) Stanley Mansfield, Royal Goff (captain), and John Kamerer; (back row) James Eddy, Anthony Thatcher, Philip Babcock, Robert Mansfield, and Joseph Kamerer.

The Darlington Milkmaids (formerly the Rehoboth Milkmaids) posed in 1940, the year they won the Rhode Island Women's Soft Ball Championship. From left to right are as follows: (front row) Rita Vincent, Arline Anderson, Hilda Berghman, Martha Richmond, Alberta Peck, and Louise Arnold; (back row) Marion Lyon, Anita Rousseau, Helen Berghman, Ora Rousseau, Raymond Barrie (team manager), Frank Potter (coach), Dorothy Forsberg, Wilhemina Corey, Rose Rousseau, and Ella Lyon.

In 1935, a group of young Rehoboth boys (ages 13-16) were dared by boys at Bristol Aggie School to take them on in baseball. The Rehoboth boys responded by forming a team of their own called the Rehoboth Tigers, which never experienced a single losing season. From left to right are as follows: (seated) Mickey Byers, Wally Davis, Albert Rousseau, Benny Vincent, Ray Kindberg, Joe Carpenter, Eddy Arvidison, and Benny Violette; (standing) Johnnie Gifford, George Sousa, and Eddy Poloquin.

A Rehoboth group (including the Hass, Read, and Barney families) escape town and hit the beach in August 1932.

The Rehoboth Antiquarian Society Clambake of 1930 was held at its traditional Goff Memorial

This colorful pageant, entitled *Anawan Rock* and written by Rev. Henry E. Oxnard, was held in Goff Memorial Hall on September 1, 1920. Space limitation does not permit identification here, but all of the participants were Rehoboth residents.

Hall location.

This Parade of the Holy Ghost Brotherhood of Charity, Blanding Road, took place c. 1941-42 as part of the annual Holy Ghost Brotherhood Festival, started in 1925 by Matthew Amaral, a representative of Rehoboth's increasingly large population of Portuguese farmers. The event, which is held to the present day in Rehoboth, was established to celebrate the traditional Holy Ghost Feast Day remembered from the Old Country. The three attractive young women at center are, from left to right, Florence (DeRosa) Fernandes, Emily (Joaquin) Pacheco, and Irene (Amaral) Silva.

Another 1940s view of the Holy Ghost Brotherhood Parade shows it making its way eastward on Route 44, approaching the Kozy Nook Tavern.

Rehoboth: Chapter Three
Tilling the Soil

The Atkinson-Cushing farm, bordered by Pine and Hillside Avenues, is shown here c. 1910 at strawberry harvest time. Samuel Atkinson's operation was a significant one; he employed so many strawberry pickers that a house was erected on his property for their use. The house still stands as a private residence (Milton and Minna Hall, a well-known Rehoboth couple, lived there as newlyweds).

Rehoboth farmer George W. Holden stands alongside his market wagon, *c.* 1890. The horses are "Kitty" and "Jerry." The Pierce name appearing on the side of the wagon indicates that it once belonged to George's great-grandfather, Samuel L. Pierce.

Rehoboth farmers Isador Demers and Frank Horton pick up grain, *c.* 1915, at East Providence's Watchamoket Square. For many years, the square was the retail center of East Providence. Its demise as a crucial retail area came in 1929, when construction of the new Washington Bridge redirected commercial traffic to present-day Route 44 in East Providence.

The Harold A. Goff farm on Perryville Road is shown here in 1890. Four generations of Goffs resided here until the farm ceased operations in the 1960s. The original house, to the left, has undergone many changes over the years and is the present-day Perryville Inn. The enormous barn to the right, torn down in 1958, occupied the site of the present-day Rehoboth Country Club.

By 1915, the year this photograph was taken, Rehoboth farmers Will Bowen, Ralph Horton, and Harold Horton were still using oxen to draw heavy loads (in this case, probably cord wood for winter storage). The children seated atop the cart have not been identified.

These folks are taking a rest from pitching hay at the Frank Horton Farm, Rehoboth Village, c. 1910. Haying was an important component of Rehoboth farming.

Frank Veader plows with a two-horse hitch on his family's Pleasant Street farm in south Rehoboth, c. 1920s. The house in the background is the former Albernaz farmhouse.

In 1898, William "Billy" Viall, who was born in Rehoboth, established a dairy business called Broadway Dairy in nearby East Providence.

From its humble beginning described above, William Viall's Broadway Dairy—which changed its name to W.C. Viall's Dairy early in the company's history—grew into a thriving business that employed some one hundred people and had forty-five trucks making milk deliveries in both Rhode Island and Massachusetts. In 1924, Viall moved milking operations to Rehoboth, to a farm on Broad Street (the present-day Hass Farm). The actual milk processing plant remained in East Providence.

Pictured here is the Viall dairy's new Rehoboth site, c. mid-1920s (the little girl is William Viall's youngest daughter, Ella). Although the dairy was a commercial venture, Viall so immaculately maintained the farm and surrounding grounds that it became a showplace which actually attracted visitors from neighboring areas. Some time later, Viall started a second farm on Providence Street in south Rehoboth. After Viall's death in 1943, his daughter Elizabeth successfully ran the dairy until she sold it in 1962.

This early photograph of the Thomas W. Carpenter farm (later the Murray farm) was taken long before it was eventually demolished in 1981, when the Bristol County Savings bank of Taunton built their Rehoboth branch on the site.

Situated for many years at the intersection of Blanding Road and Summer Street in Rehoboth, the Kinne Farm, pictured here in the 1940s, was a sizeable, magnificent dairy operation whose milk trucks were a familiar sight throughout Providence. Tragically, the farm was destroyed in a raging 1953 fire. The dairy operation never regained its former prominence.

Picking up potatoes at the Horton Farm, October 1941. From left to right are Frank Horton, Albert Rousseau, unknown, Steve Soares, and Ralph Horton (Frank's son).

Gentleman farmer Stuart Aldrich, brother-in-law to John D. Rockefeller, holds one of his prize Guernsey bulls at the magnificent Aldrich show farm. In the farm's immaculate surroundings, Aldrich perfected a strain of Golden Guernsey cattle. He sold the farm in 1949 to another cattle breeder. In time, breeding operations ceased at the farm, and the site eventually became home to the present-day Crestwood Country Club (Crestwood's main clubhouse occupies one of the former Aldrich barns).

Silage corn is being "put in" on the DeMattos farm on Summer Street in 1940. The portable engine to the right (known as a "one lunger" because of its single piston) was an older method of powering the cutter; by this time, the more modern method on many farms involved utilizing a tractor with a flywheel.

Rehoboth: Chapter Four

Teaching Our Tots, Tending Our Souls

Located at the corner of School and Summer Streets in Rehoboth Village (and known as the "Little Red School House"), this early nineteenth-century schoolhouse is shown here in 1917. Standing, from left to right, are Alice Nock, Ruth (Parker) Ramspott, Mabel Nock, Gladys Goff, Ralph Nock, Ralph Horton (smaller boy standing in front of larger boy, Clyde Nichols), Samuel Cumberland, and unknown. Today, extensively changed in its appearance, the old school stands as a private residence.

By 1840, there were twenty-two schools in Rehoboth (by 1847 these twenty-two schools were combined into fifteen school districts). Included among these early schools was the Bliss School on Homestead Avenue in north Rehoboth, pictured here c. 1880. This school was eventually closed because of a lack of pupils in this section of town.

This class inside the Blanding School, at the corner of Broad and Wilmarth Bridge Road, was photographed c. 1904. See Anna (Hass) Morgan's *Memoirs* for a delightful first-hand account of her turn-of-the-century experiences in this little one-room schoolhouse. Due to the advent of the town's larger, newly consolidated Anawan School, Blanding School, like many of the town's other one-room schools, closed its doors in 1930. The building still stands and presently serves as the meeting place of the Holy Ghost Brotherhood of Charity.

Blanding School students play outside the school building at recess, c. 1920s.

One of the town's earliest school buses, pictured here c. 1923, was purchased by the town to transport students to the Pleasant Street school in Rehoboth, which was constructed in 1922 at a cost of $22,000 and was the town's first consolidated school.

Pictured here is Hornbine School's class of 1909. The teacher standing to left is Ethel Stevens from Brockton. Among the students pictured are children from the Magan, Padnorse, Rose, Bettencourt, and Ellis families.

Driven by Harold Horton (pictured here) between the years 1934 and 1947, this old schoolbus became a familiar sight in town during its long tenure and was jokingly referred to as the "chicken coop" by Rehoboth residents because of its squarish resemblance to a henhouse.

Standing across from Rehoboth's famous Hornbine School is the Hornbine Baptist Church (also called the First Free Baptist Church), constructed in 1753 and pictured here c. 1890, long before Hornbine Road was even paved. The little church, which still holds services, was started by thirty individuals (led by the Rev. Daniel Martin) who had separated—likely for reasons of theological dispute—from the main Baptist Church in Swansea.

Rehoboth's Congregational Church, pictured here about 1900, was built in Rehoboth Village in 1839 at a total cost of $3,800. It was the third Congregational church built within present-day Rehoboth boundaries (replacing the Yellow Meeting House in the Village Cemetery, which had been used as a church since 1773). Note the carriage sheds, which were destroyed in the twister of 1927.

Built on Plain Street and dedicated in 1834, the First Christian Church (formerly called the Oak Swamp Church) began, in 1842, to lean toward the Millerite doctrine (an apocalyptic New England movement that predicted the imminent destruction of the earth). This offended many of the elder members of the congregation, who subsequently left the church. After the Millerite doctrines declined in popularity later in the nineteenth century, the church struggled with its denominational identity. By the 1940s, the congregation had entirely fragmented, and the church closed it doors.

No longer standing, the first and only nearby Catholic parish church available to Rehoboth's Catholics was Our Lady of Mount Carmel, which stood just over the town line in Seekonk. Pictured here c. 1950s, the church was constructed in 1904 and, sadly, was demolished in 1982. It was replaced by a new, larger church building (built just slightly to the west of the original).

Rehoboth: Chapter Five

Turning Back the Clock

The Old Goff Inn, dating back to the late eighteenth century, was a stagecoach stop, tavern, and inn on the Providence to Taunton stagecoach route (at the time, the coach trip from Providence to Taunton took a full day). Owned by Rehoboth's well-known Goff family, the inn was torn down in 1885, and the site was donated by Darius Goff to Rehoboth's newly formed Antiquarian Society. The Society subsequently built Rehoboth's first Goff Memorial Hall on the site.

The original Goff Memorial Hall was constructed in 1885 and burned down by a lightning strike in 1911 (it was later replaced on the same Bay State Road site by the present-day brick building). The Memorial Hall housed a schoolroom, a public meeting-hall, a library, and an Antiquarian Room.

Pictured here c. 1900 is the Antiquarian Room mentioned above. It is laden with Rehoboth-relevant relics that would later form the core of the Carpenter Museum Collection.

The early-nineteenth-century Pierce Homestead, which still stands at the corner of Brook and Moulton Streets (known as "Coffin Corner"), served as Daniel and Susannah Pierce's home and place of business. The most notable of their mercantile activities was the coffin-building and undertaking business operated here by Daniel and his son Lloyd. Interestingly, famous news anchor Walter Cronkite's great grandmother (a Pierce) was born in this house.

Susan Pierce (the daughter of Daniel and Susannah) is pictured here, c. 1890, standing in front of the house that her parents built for her directly across from their own Coffin Corner house (pictured above) when she married in 1859. To the left is Susan's son Harvey. Pierce descendants have occupied the home to the present day.

An early Rehoboth clambake run by Mr. Peleg Francis, whose increasingly popular Francis Farm clambakes were undoubtedly so successful because Mr. Francis had found a way to buy clams at only $1 a bushel (today a bushel would cost $90!). This allowed Francis Farm to offer its many customers a complete clam dinner (which also included sweet potatoes, tripe, brownbread, watermelons, and corn) for the mere price of 50¢!

Colonel Thomas Carpenter, a wealthy landowner and leader of the Rehoboth militia during the American Revolution, constructed this Bay State Road home in 1750 (the house was actually built around an earlier core residential structure). The house (still-standing) features an exquisite Georgian-style interior typical of the urban mansions of the wealthy mercantile class in Providence and Boston.

Because of the many additions that were later added to this building (the old post office on Bay State Road in Rehoboth Village), it looks far different in this *c.* 1905 photograph than it does today. This post office became a private residence when the new post office was built on Rehoboth Commons in 1984.

The trolley (operated by the Providence and Taunton Street Railway Company) that ran from Providence to Taunton along what is now Route 44 was established in 1897 and ran until the automobile gradually put it out of business in 1927. In Anna (Hass) Morgan's *Memoirs* (edited by Charles Robinson and published by The Rehoboth Antiquarian Society in 1997), it is noted that, after much debate, Senator George Nelson Goff persuaded the promoters of the trolley line to establish a detour through Rehoboth Village.

Mrs. Irene Hass, mother of Anna (Hass) Morgan, stands proudly by her new 1/2-ton truck. Her grandsons, Alfred and Carlos (Anna's sons), hold the Hass family signboard that will be mounted on the side of the truck. The photograph was taken at the Hass farm on Summer Street in Rehoboth, c. 1926.

In this 1902 photograph, the numerous parked buggies at Frank H. Horton's Rehoboth residence (the turn-of-the-century equivalent to hoards of parked cars) suggest a social function or funeral within the home.

This view of Bay State Road in the early part of the century looks very different today. When the photograph was taken, this particular point in the road was an important trolley stop known as Nichols Crossing. Note to the right the small trolley waiting station, which—despite the trolley's closing in 1927—stood until the 1940s.

This early photograph of Locust Street from the north shows how different things looked at the turn of the century. The Carpenter Museum, which today stands precisely where the small shed (to the left behind church) appears here, had yet to be built.

Showing off the new family car in the summer of 1933 are, from left to right, Fred Bowen, Barbara (Horton) Vandenberg, Joan (Horton) Olson, May Horton, Bimi Bowen, and Fred Bowen Sr. Proudly seated in the new '33 Ford is Harold Horton.

Bob Trim, a carpenter by trade but also the town's most prolific and important Rehoboth genealogist and historian, is pictured here in the summer of 1940 showing off a new truck acquired by the Rehoboth Fire Department, for which he was also a volunteer firefighter.

In 1934, an errant (and likely drunk) driver drove his car through the Rehoboth home of Louis Demers, located on Route 44 near the intersection of Wilmarth Bridge Road. Louis (standing closest to the house) was asleep in an upstairs bedroom at the time of the incident and, unlike his wrecked house, managed to escape injury.

A once-popular event in Rehoboth was the annual soapbox derby, which was sponsored by the Rehoboth Lions Club. The event is pictured here in 1950 in south Rehoboth on the very high hill at the intersection of Providence and Mason Streets. The man to the right (facing the camera, wearing a hat) is Frank Veader. His son Alfred sits in the car to the left of Frank.

An early aerial shot (c. 1940) of Rehoboth Village highlights many features—architectural and otherwise—that have changed between then and now. For instance, note Frank Horton's sizeable dairy farm (at the lower right), which was then still in operation (years later the barn became Fletcher School and subsequently a showpiece private residence). Note also the Congregational Church (at center), which at this time lacked Fellowship Hall. To the rear right of the church are turkey pens—located on what is now the site of the Carpenter Museum. Additionally, the small building to the far right edge of the photograph was Rehoboth's post office at the time this photograph was taken (it is now a private home; a much larger, modern post office stands elsewhere in town).

Swansea: Chapter One

The Clank of the Coin

John Brown Luther established the Luther Store in 1818 at the corner of Maple Street and Old Warren Road (sometimes still called by its old name, Milford Road). John died five years later, and the store, which sold general merchandise, was taken over by his brother, Joseph Gardner Luther. The Luther Store became one of the town's principal commercial establishments, where a large number of townsfolk gathered to discuss local happenings. Upon Joseph's death, his son, Joseph Jr., also the town's treasurer and tax collector, continued to run the business. The Luther store finally closed in 1903 and presently stands as the museum of the Swansea Historical Society.

In 1815, three years prior to the establishment of the Luther Store by his relative John, James Luther established the Luther Tavern (on the opposite side of the same junction where the Luther Store would be built in 1818). It served as a stagecoach stop between Providence and Fall River, and it is said that only non-alcoholic drinks were served here.

Israel Brayton built a store at the corner of Main and Elm in 1815. He gathered many locally produced products from around the countryside, such as locally made shoes and cotton cloth woven in Swansea homes, and in turn he shipped them to faraway places like Boston. In return he received such exotic goods as rum, spices, china, and other wares that otherwise would have been unavailable to Swansea residents. The business thrived for many years.

Mason Barney built his first large three-master in 1803, when he was merely twenty years old. Unbeknownst to the Bristol colonel who had contracted him to build the ship, young Barney, as he admitted years later, had accepted the job without knowing how to use even simple, basic tools. He pulled off the immense task by hiring, directing, and organizing the labor of others, and it is here that he discovered his greatest talent. Over the next half-century, by employing and directing as many as 175 men at a time, the soon-wealthy Barney built some 137 ships in his bustling shipyard on the banks of the Palmer River. His fine boats included slave ships, whaling vessels, and gun boats for the government during the Mexican War. The advent of iron vessels and a financial panic in 1858 ended this remarkable Swansea enterprise.

A milk man's rig is shown here c. 1890-1900. Probably by about 1920, the horse-drawn milk-cart was a thing of the past in Swansea and surrounding towns.

Swansea's Case Hotel was built on the site of a former inn run by the Gray family. When the inn burned down in the mid-nineteenth-century, Joseph Case, who had been working at the inn and who had married Eliza Gray, constructed and ran the Case Hotel. The hotel was popular for its well-known dining room. Eventually, it was turned into the Eliza Gray Case Home (for widows and orphan daughters of retired Episcopal clergy) by Miss Mary A. Case, Joseph's daughter.

R.C. Gray's blacksmith shop on Main Street in Swansea is shown here c. 1910. The woman standing to left is Fanny Wood, who held what was an unusual town position for a woman at the time—she was Post Master of Swansea from c. 1900 until about 1925. She apparently took this national appointment very seriously, as she used her own funds to build a post office immediately adjacent to the blacksmith shop pictured here.

This is the Leonard Sherman Shingle Mill, located at the end of a lane on the east side of Hortonville Road, at the turn of the century. Pictured from left to right are Leonard Sherman, William Hathaway, and Mrs. Leonard Sherman (seated in the buggy).

The Swansea Print Works occupied a site that had seen various commercial activity beginning about 1815, including a gristmill, a paper mill, a bleachery, and a dye works. When the Swansea Print Works was finally established on the site (pictured here early in the century), it quickly

became known for its very high quality textile printing. This fine, quality-conscious company was eventually bought out by the Swan Finishing Company, at which point operations were transferred to Fall River.

An oyster house on the Coles River, c. 1910-20. From the earliest settlement until c. 1930, Swansea had a thriving oyster industry. Oysters were taken across the river by rowboat to Fall River, where they were loaded onto the Fall River Line steamer and shipped to New York's finest hotels by the following day.

Cummings Store (left), shown here c. early 1900s, was located in Swansea's Hortonville section. Hortonville was the site of one of the area's first cotton mills (1804), predating even the mills of Fall River. The Hortonville section was also an important small industry area for many years. To the right is Liberty Hall and Chapel.

H.G. Wilbur's soda fountain at Swasey's Corner in Swansea is shown here c. 1920. The business, owned by the Wilbur family (who also had a business in Boston), was known for its attractive glass storefront and beautiful marbletop soda fountain. Since it stood across the street from the large pond at the Swansea dam, the business served hot chocolate to shivering ice-skaters for many years. A small grocery store occupies the building today.

The Luther Store (see p. 53) had always stood just a few feet from the crossroads. However, during the Depression, the people of Swansea enlisted the help of Mrs. Louis Howe (center), a Fall River resident whose husband was an advisor to Franklin D. Roosevelt, to get the store moved farther back from the road as a WPA project. The reason for the building's distancing from the crossroads was the ever-increasing automobile traffic of the 1930s. At left is Maude Parlin, the project architect. At right is Daniel Wetherell.

J. Borge & Sons Sand and Gravel Company (the first large gravel company in the area) was a very successful Swansea firm founded in 1927. Large contract jobs—such as hauling gravel to Newport for the Navy during World War II and hauling the gravel for Swansea's Route 6—made the business very prosperous. The company continued its operations until the 1970s, when Almacs purchased its land.

These trucks belonged to the well-known Reise's dairy, c. 1938-39. Their trucks not only became a familiar site in Swansea, but also in Fall River, Rehoboth, and other areas serviced by this prosperous dairy. The firm closed in 1966.

Swansea: Chapter Two

Laughter and Leisure

A Swansea family at around the turn of the century enjoys a bountiful clambake—a frequent summer ritual among many Swansea residents at this time.

The Swansea Brass Band reached its heyday in the 1890s—about the time this photograph was taken. The band was a familiar sight at parades and other town functions and often played free outdoor concerts. (In other words, entertainment for town residents in the days before private entertainments like televisions and VCRs was much more public and collective.)

A group of Swansea and Fall River residents enjoy a sightseeing tour in New York City, probably c. 1917. The tour was arranged by Swansea resident Orrin Gardner, a teacher who frequently arranged such tours for Swansea-area residents.

These pageant participants were photographed during the town's 250th anniversary celebration in 1919. Massasoit (center) is played by Francis Gardner, chairman of the board of selectmen. The other two pageant actors are North Swansea resident William Jordan (left, playing Myles Standish), and Swansea physician Dr. John D. Hilton (right, playing Edward Winslow).

Mrs. Elizabeth Case Stevens observes a pageant during Swansea's 250th anniversary celebration in 1919 (it was supposed to have taken place in 1917 but was delayed because of World War I). Alongside her, to the left, is Army General Nelson Myles, who was a descendant of the Reverend John Myles, one of the principal founders of Swansea.

This minstrel show, consisting of Swansea women in blackface, was not considered "politically incorrect" in the 1920s. Such Swansea performances, popular in the days before television and other modern entertainments, were put on by women's groups and other groups in places like the town hall and the Grange Hall (probably the location pictured here).

If these Swansea women do not appear to be too attractive, it is because they are actually Swansea men. They are dressed for a Swansea Grange production put on about 1919-20. The not-so-lovely young "lady" to the far left is actually the (male) chairman of Swansea's Board of Selectmen.

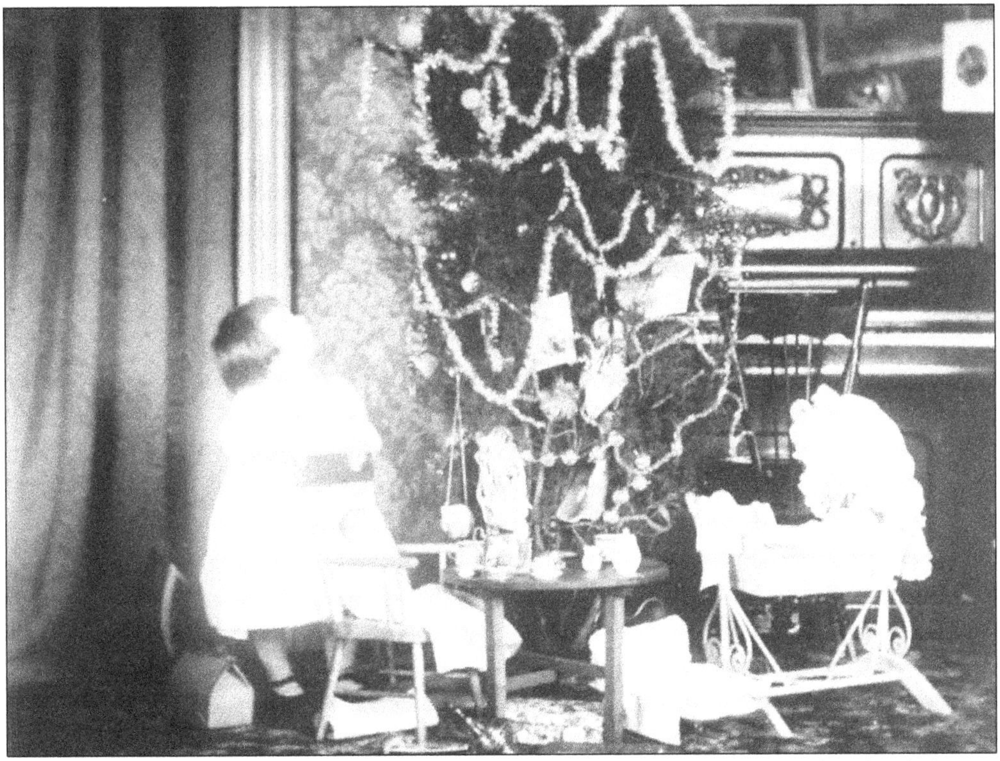

Rachel Gardner, c. 1912, feels tiny alongside the towering Christmas tree in her family home, located at 1129 Gardner's Neck Road in Swansea. Her father built the house c. 1909 and Rachel, now much taller, still lives there to the present day.

Swansea resident Leyland Buffington (whose grandson eventually became a well-known stage and television actor in Hollywood) is pictured here clowning for the camera about 1890. He was evidently canoeing that afternoon on Swansea's Coles River.

In 1925, this group of Swansea-area residents took a sight-seeing tour to Washington, D.C.

A warm welcome home was given to returning Swansea veterans of World War I, c. 1918.

Swansea: Chapter Three
People of Prominence

Starting out as a worker in a livery stable on Benefit Street in Providence, James Birch followed the 49ers out to California during the Gold Rush of 1849. Within four years he became the founder and president of a multi-million dollar stagecoach company in Sacramento. In 1852, Birch married Swansea resident Julia A.B. Chace and moved back east, where he and his new wife built a mansion on Main Street in Swansea (the present-day Stevens Home for Boys). Birch also moved his business operations (which now involved the promotion of trans-Continental coach mail) to Swansea. On a business trip in 1857, Mr. Birch was lost at sea when his ship went down off the coast of South Carolina. Julia eventually remarried (see next page).

In 1858, Julia Birch married Frank Shaw Stevens, her late husband's friend and business associate. Julia and Frank (along with Julia's son by Birch) lived in the Swansea mansion built by Birch until 1871, when Julia died at a young age, leaving Frank Shaw Stevens a widower with a young stepson.

After Julia's death in 1871, Frank Shaw Stevens remarried in 1873, this time to Swansea resident Elizabeth Richmond Case (see the top of p. 71), whose father ran a local hotel. Over the years, as his invested wealth continued to grow, Stevens became the town's leading philanthropist and benefactor, contributing money for, among other things, construction of the town hall. Upon his death, he bequeathed $40,000 for the construction of Christ Church and the town library.

Elizabeth Richmond Case was the second wife of Frank Shaw Stevens. Mrs. Stevens, who died in 1930, actively continued the philanthropy of her husband after his death in 1891, using her own money to finance the Stevens School and the Joseph Case High School.

In 1693, Samuel Gardner purchased Mattapoiset Neck. His five great grandsons (pictured here c. 1850, when they were already over seventy) inherited portions of Mattapoiset and established their homes and families on the Neck, leading to a Gardner population explosion (one brother alone had ten sons; another had five sons and eight daughters). Hence, Mattapoiset Neck eventually became better known as Gardner's Neck—the name it still carries today. From left to right they are as follows: (seated) Preserved, Job, and Peleg; (standing) Alexander and Samuel.

Joseph Luther Jr. was heir to one of Swansea's foremost nineteenth-century mercantile operations (see p. 53 for further information).

Not as notable as some of the people pictured previously, but certainly an attractive and fashionable Swansea couple, Mr. and Mrs. Nathaniel Horton are pictured here around the time of the First World War.

Swansea: Chapter Four

The Pastoral Past

The lonely ruin of a windmill, probably dating to the end of the eighteenth century, is shown here about 1900, long after it had been abandoned. Known as "Potter's Mill," it was an early gristmill on the Coles River (near the former Almacs complex on Rt. 6) owned by the Potter family.

Swansea's turn-of-the-century agricultural flavor is captured well in this photograph of the period.

The Abner Slade Farm is pictured here about the turn of the century, complete with Holstein cows. Abner Slade was a very successful farmer, tanner, and even banker (he was director of the Fall River National Bank). The farm's lovely Victorian house, seen here in background, stood at the corner of Stevens Road and Bark Street. Eventually, Abner moved off the farm, and his son-in-law, Charles Chase, took up residence there until about 1900. The house burned down during the early part of the century.

To the right in this c. turn-of-the-century photograph is Swansea farmer Philander Wilbur; standing to the left is Philander's grandson, Lewis H. Gray, who became Swansea's first mailman when the town established rural free delivery in the early part of the century.

Workers clear field stones, c. 1890s, at the Leland Gardner Farm, one of several very successful area farms owned by the Gardner family at the turn of the century. Swansea's farmers were haunted by field stones, which continuously popped out of New England's rocky soil and thwarted the plow. After clearing, farmers put the stones to good use in constructing fine stone walls like the one pictured here.

Unlike Swansea's working farms, Cedar Lane Farm was a "gentleman's farm" used as a lovely summer residence by Wallace R. Lane (a corporate lawyer from Chicago) and his wife, Swansea resident Gertrude Gardner, during the 1930s and '40s.

Cedar Lane Farm, pictured above, featured Guernsey cattle. Mr. Lane ran the farm meticulously, continuously improving his stock by breeding his cows to the finest Guernsey bulls. Pictured here is herdsman Antone Medeiros, one of Mr. Lane's large staff. The farm was sold in 1948 to Ian M. Walker; it continued as a show farm for Guernsey cattle until 1960.

Swansea: Chapter Five

Moving About

Gray's corner in Swansea is shown here around 1890, obviously before any of Swansea's streets were paved.

Swansea's Main Street is shown here in a view looking west at the turn of the century.

This is the exact same view as the one above, ninety-six years later (1996). Notice the same house still standing to the left.

Horses were a familiar sight on Swansea's roads prior to the advent of the automobile. So many horses, of course, meant a good deal of street clean-up, which was mostly done by rain and traffic.

With the advent of rural free delivery c. 1903, carrier Lewis H. Gray and his mail cart—one of two servicing the town—became a familiar sight on Swansea's streets. Prior to rural free delivery, townspeople had to pick up their own mail in town.

At the turn of the century, trains ran through Swansea every half hour en route between Providence and Fall River. Via train, people from surrounding cities like Providence now had access to summer resort areas like Swansea's Ocean Grove. The train bridge pictured here—Lee's River Bridge—was in heavy use until its destruction in the Hurricane of 1938.

During the late 19th and early 20th centuries, steam trains (later electrified) like the one pictured in the previous photograph made frequent stops at the Souh Swansea station pictured here. As indicated, the train ran between Full River and Providence every half hour and was known as the "Snake Line" becauseof its very winding course.

This was one of the open trolleys that ran, beginning in 1901, from city hall in Fall River to Market Square in Providence, stopping in Swansea along the way.

Two trolley conductors take a break at the Swansea stop. The conductor to left is Ralph West, who worked for the line for many years until automobile competition forced the line into bankruptcy in the early 1920s. At right is Andy Herbert.

A road gang with steam roller is shown here c. 1920. At this time, Swansea did not have its own road crews and equipment but rather contracted outside firms to do the work. At left is Charles Williams, overseeing his workers.

This road construction took place in 1935 on Hailes Hill Road in Swansea.

Swansea: Chapter Six
Keeping Our Faith, Expanding Our Knowledge

The establishment of Swansea's First Baptist Church was actually synonymous with the town's founding. The church boasts the oldest continuous Baptist congregation in Massachusetts (the fifth oldest in New England). The congregation was first started in 1663 by Reverend John Myles in present-day Barrington, after his Baptist preaching had brought persecution in other parts of Massachusetts (including Rehoboth). In 1667, in spite of their intolerance toward some of Reverend Myles' Baptist views, Plymouth Colony finally granted Myles and his congregation a tract of land for the establishment of a town and his church. Myles had originally come from Swansea, Wales; hence, Swansea is the name he gave to the site of this new settlement.

The First Christian Congregational Church—commonly called "The White Church"—first held services in 1680, making it one of the oldest churches in New England (in terms of the congregation, that is; the building pictured here is not the original but was built in 1833). It is believed that this was the first New England Church to admit all Christians regardless of creed. This early picture shows carriage sheds (now gone) to right.

St. Francis Xavier Church stood on Old Barneyville Road. The church was first established in the early 1800s as a Baptist Church, at the prompting of nearby shipyard owner Mason Barney (see p. 55). His workers were partying too heartily, and he thought the church would calm them. The church fell into disuse after the shipyard's closing and was eventually taken over by Catholics. It was damaged badly in the 1938 hurricane and no longer stands.

The parishioners of St. Francis Xavier Church posed for this photograph c. early 1900s.

The Bark Street School is shown here at around the turn of the century. In 1905, the structure was replaced by a second school (which later became the town hall annex).

Students of the Swansea Village School, one of the very few early schoolhouses to feature two classrooms instead of one, posed for this photograph in 1904. The large number of bicycles recalls a time when students had to walk or bicycle to class, as certain municipal services like school bus service were still years in the future. The Stevens School currently stands on this site at the head of Main Street.

A class, pictured in 1904, poses with their teacher at the Swansea Village School. Note the two separate entrances, one for girls and one for boys.

Students from the North Swansea School are shown here *c.* 1890. The fact that the students are pictured off school grounds carrying a large American flag strongly suggests that they are observing Memorial Day—at this time a holiday widely celebrated (because of the proximity of the Civil War) by all of the area's schoolchildren, who ceremoniously paraded to local cemeteries and placed flowers on the graves of soldiers.

This is the interior of the Gardner School on Ocean Grove Avenue, *c.* 1910. The teacher seated at the upper left is Olive Brown Grimes. Calvin Gardner, who grew up to be the executive secretary to the board of selectmen, is seated in the row closest to the camera. Currently, the old Gardner School building is utilized as the American Legion Meeting Hall.

In 1935, students at the Joseph Case School put on this spirited production of Gilbert and Sullivan's *H.M.S. Pinafore*.

Swansea's Case High School band rehearses for an impending football game against Dighton High School, c. 1940. The woman at right (leading the band) is Miss Ruth B. Eddy, supervisor of music in the Swansea public schools. After this brief practice, the band would be transported to the game in the 1920s-style school bus pictured in the background; at this time, it was one of the town's first and oldest public school buses still in commission.

Swansea: Chapter Seven

Going to the Grove

The bathing beach at Ocean Grove, c. 1915, at the Coles River. Located in the plains of South Swansea, the area was developed by the Wilbur Land Company into a summer home and resort area beginning about 1906. It catered to blue collar working people unable to afford the more posh seasonal resort areas of New England. By its heyday in the 1930s and '40s, Ocean Grove also attracted numerous non-residential day and evening visitors from urban areas like Fall River and Providence, who came to enjoy popular entertainments like a famous ballroom featuring big bands. Ocean Grove eventually died out as a summer entertainment area by the 1950s. Thereafter, it grew primarily as a year-round residential community.

This was a typical c. 1910–15 Ocean Grove summer house—small and affordable for its blue collar occupants. Most Ocean Grove houses were, like this one, quaint cottages with equally quaint names. This one was called "Idle Hour" and was owned by Edith Cornell.

The very tiny size of many of Ocean Grove's summer residences is made clear by the overflowing porch pictured here. This house may have had a "Pleasant View" of the Coles River, as its sign delineates, but living here was undoubtedly a bit of a "squeeze" for its numerous occupants.

Summer life in the Grove included daily visits to the B.A. Chace Store—pictured here about 1915—where residents got their groceries, ice cream, gossip, and mail (the store doubled as the area's post office).

The Bluffs was an amusement center situated at the center of Ocean Grove. This large building hosted big bands, a famous ballroom, roller skating, bowling, food concessions, and many other fun diversions. This very popular entertainment center drew countless summer visitors from surrounding urban areas like Fall River and Providence. The Bluffs reached its heyday in the 1930s and '40s and declined shortly thereafter. Since the early 1970s, the Bluffs building has served as the town's Senior Citizens Center.

Beachgoers at Ocean Grove were not exclusively area residents. The folks pictured here c. 1920 escaped hot cities like Fall River by hopping a train that brought them to Ocean Grove for a day at the beach—an inexpensive weekend diversion for blue collar families before and during the Depression years.

Ocean Grove's close proximity to Mount Hope Bay rendered it especially vulnerable to the Hurricane of 1938, which struck with no prior warning. The horrific leveling wreaked by this powerful storm is evident in this photograph. In a way, the hurricane symbolized the beginning of the end for Ocean Grove as an entertainment center (by the 1950s, as indicated earlier, the Grove would die out as a center of summer amusement and diversion, although it continued on as a residential area).

Dighton: Chapter One
Trade and Industry

These employees of the Dighton Furnace Company were photographed c. 1880s. Although the back of the photograph gives the location as North Dighton, the mill was located just over the Taunton line, though it was largely staffed by Dighton men. A strike at the factory caused a riot in North Dighton Village in 1886. In 1907 the business burned down in a terrible fire, taking with it two adjacent homes. The loss was estimated at $60,000, a sizeable sum in 1907.

These people, photographed c. 1910, were employees of the former Anchor Color and Gum Works, located where Salley Richmond Brook crosses Elm Street. The factory was the site of many previous businesses, and, by the time this photograph was taken, it was owned by the Arnold Hoffman Company of Providence.

Imperial Chemical Industries of England, at the time the world's largest chemical manufacturer, took over the Arnold Hoffman Company in 1950 as its American subsidiary. At this time, because company operations required vast amounts of water, a large dam and reservoir were

In July of 1906, four years before the employee photograph on p. 94 was taken, the Arnold Hoffman Company partially burned. It was quickly rebuilt and resumed its manufacture of water colors, soap, and corn starch products.

built alongside the factory. Although some residents were disturbed by the loss of sprawling green woods laced with rare wild flowers, the reservoir was not entirely unattractive.

These employees of the Dighton Canning Factory were photographed near the freight depot in South Dighton, c. 1900. The factory greatly benefited the farmers of the area by purchasing surplus goods. Items canned at the factory included squash, tomatoes, and beans. In 1906, the Dighton Canning Factory ceased operations and was converted by a new owner, W.W. Crossman, into a tack factory.

D.D. Andrews established his first general store in 1868. Pictured here about 1900, the store sold dry goods, groceries, and general provisions, including boots and shoes. The business expanded to such an extent that D.D. Andrews, in about 1905, moved his store out of this building and into a larger one.

The original D.D. Andrews store was converted into the town's fire station in 1910. It is shown here in 1912, draped in bunting for the town's bicentennial celebration.

After outgrowing his first store, D.D. Andrews built his new store, c. 1905, just to the east of the original. It is pictured here many years later, after several different owners and a name change in about 1945 to the Red & White Market. The store still sells groceries to the present day.

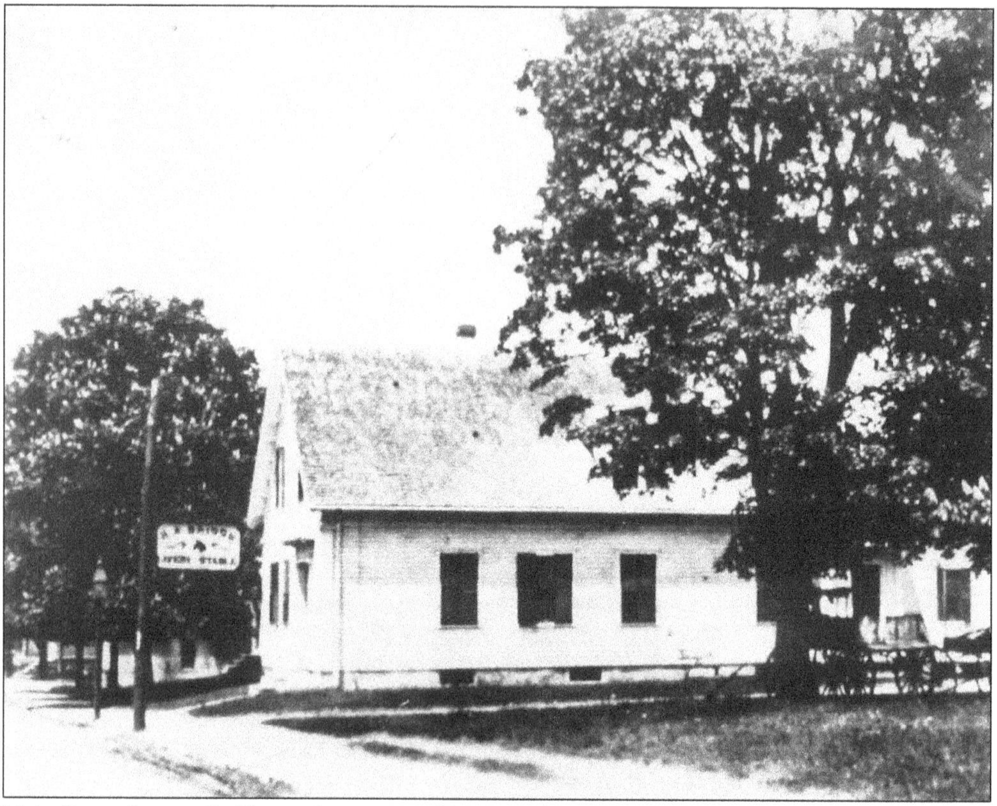

H.A. Briggs Livery Stable, at the corner of Main and County Streets in Dighton, is shown here in 1898. As indicated on the old Briggs invoice pictured below, by 1912 the stable had also begun to expand and diversify into a furniture-moving business.

Dighton, Mass. 1912

M

To H. A. BRIGGS, Dr.

LIVERY AND BOARDING STABLE.

FURNITURE MOVING AND GENERAL TEAMING.

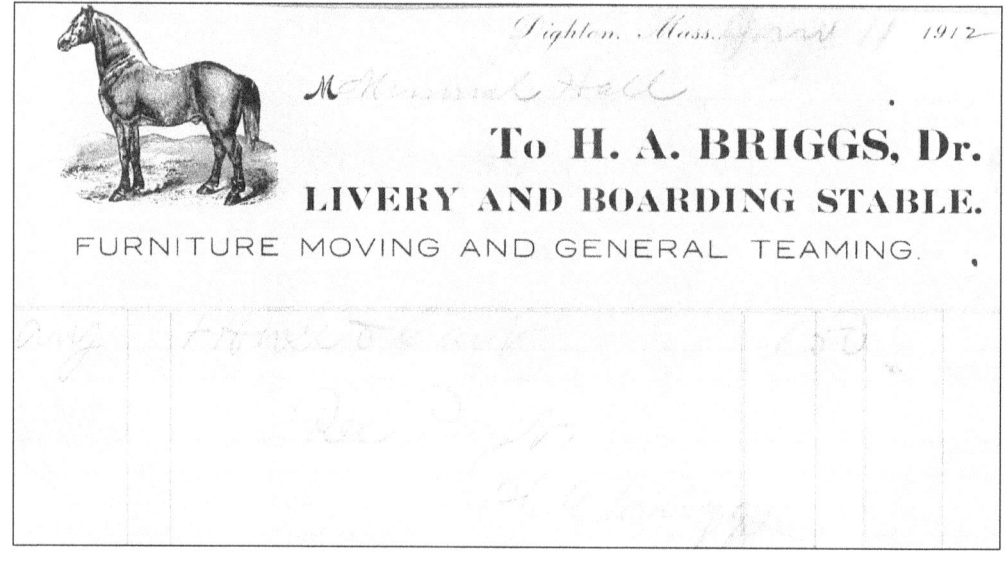

The furniture-moving aspect of the Briggs business continued to expand under H.A. Brigg's son, Lester Briggs. Eventually, the company grew into a large moving and trucking company (one of Dighton's largest companies). This 1962 photograph shows the extent to which the Brigg's fleet eventually expanded.

In the days before water pollution hindered fishing in Dighton's Taunton River, fishermen used horses and large spool-type devices to let out and draw in their nets. This photograph was taken c. 1900.

A schooner, c. 1915, is docked at the Dighton Stove Lining Company, located on the Taunton River (just north of the present Shaw's Boatyard). Schooners like this one brought in the large amounts of clay that the Dighton Stove Lining Company used in its stove linings. The company was first opened in 1874 by Gideon C. Francis and a partner and thrived for many years.

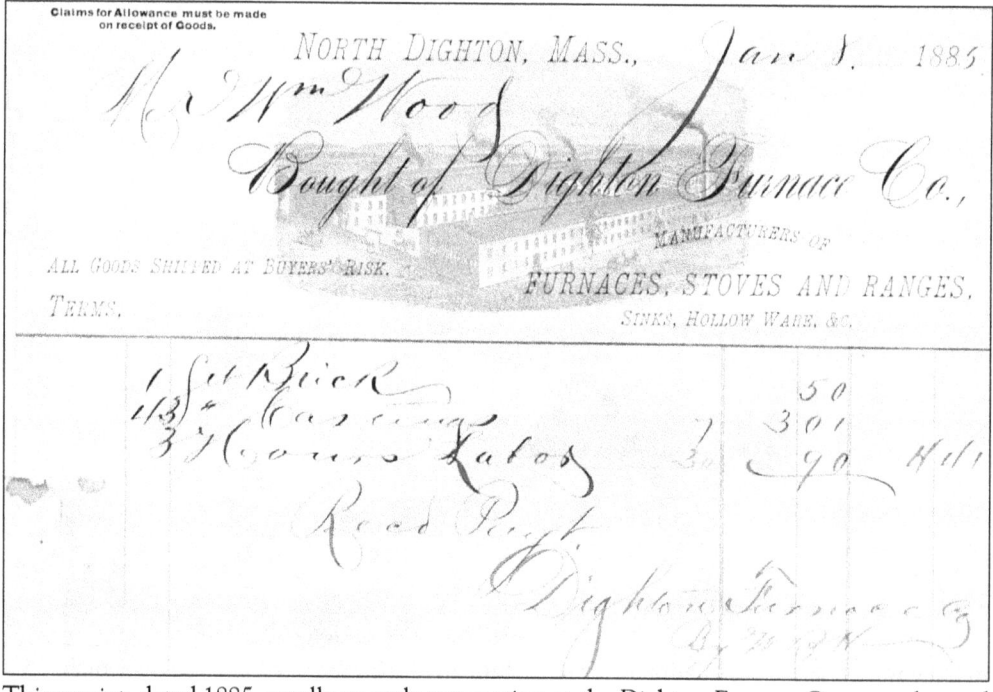

This receipt, dated 1885, recalls an early transaction at the Dighton Furnace Company located at the North Gighton/Taunton town line.

Dighton: Chapter Two
Fun and Frolic

From 1896 until 1921, Dighton Rock Park on the west bank of the Taunton River was a flourishing amusement center for both Dighton residents and city folk from Providence and Fall River, who travelled to the park via steamer and trolley. Activities included dancing, picnics, clambakes, swimming, boating, and bowling. On June 15, 1921, a raging fire entirely destroyed the park, which was never rebuilt.

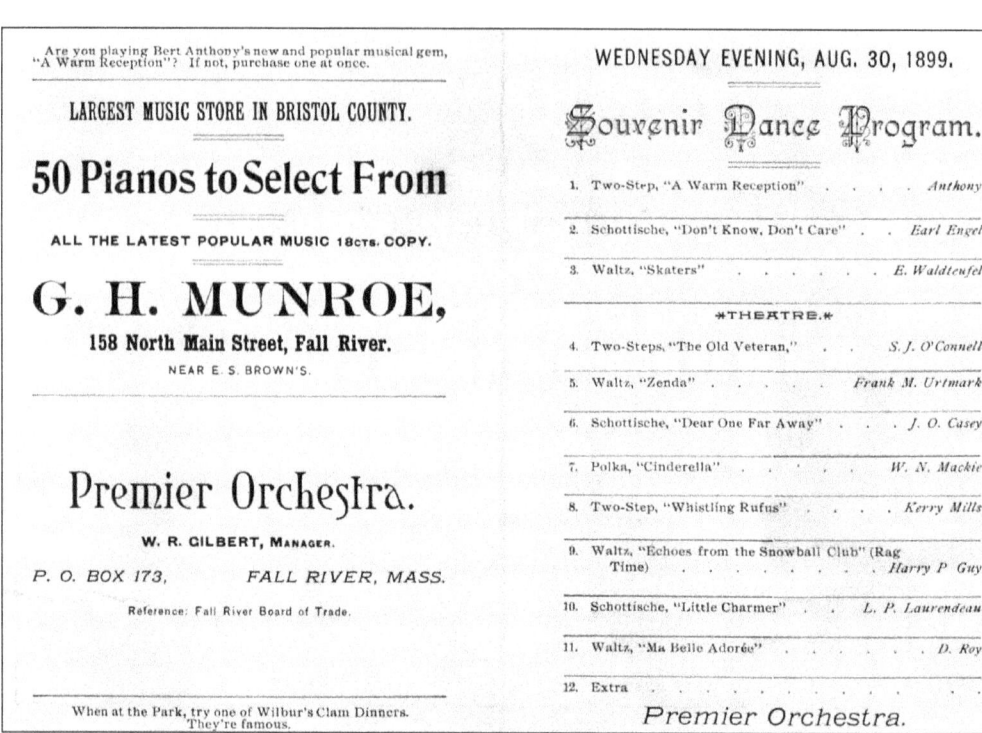

This Dighton Rock Park Dance Program was for Wednesday, August 30, 1899.

Two young ladies, c. 1890, explore Dighton Rock, a popular tourist attraction located on the east bank of the Taunton River. The enigmatic and archaeologically inconclusive carvings on the boulder have been speculatively attributed to everyone from sixteenth-century Portuguese explorers to tenth-century Viking seafarers. The mysterious rock remains a tourist attraction to the present day.

The once-beautiful Dighton Rock Park is pictured here as it burned on June 15, 1921.

This is an old view of the Dighton Yacht Club building, which once stood on the west bank of the Taunton River in Dighton. It was destroyed in the Hurricane of 1938 and has been replaced by another building on Water Street.

Shown here in this c. 1903 photograph are "Grand Army of the Republic Sons of Northern Veterans of the Civil War." "Sons" is merely a figurative term; there are actually some old Union soldiers (not just their sons) seen among this group.

In 1912, the owner of Marble's Dairy dressed up his home (in the background) with red, white, and blue bunting for the town's bicentennial celebration. In the foreground of the picture is one of Marble Dairy's milk carts.

Three Dighton bathing beauties pose for the camera, c. 1915.

This 1930 photograph shows a fisherman's three-hour catch at Pleasant Street along the Taunton River, one of the town's most popular former fishing spots. Today, because of river pollution, it would be impossible to make such a healthy Taunton River catch in a mere three hours (or probably at all, for that matter).

The three women at left were voted Dighton's Ugliest Women for 1935. Actually, kidding aside, these women are not women at all, but rather are men dressed as women for a 1935 Dighton Rock Grange skit of a shotgun wedding.

This is an early view of Dighton's Three Mile River—a lovely portion along which Dighton residents could relax with a leisurely picnic or stroll.

The interior of the Rufus Whitmarsh House is shown here around the turn of the century. In the eighteenth century, William Emery came to live in this house with Rufus because, after signing the Declaration of Independence as a Rhode Island Representative, Emery's home was burned by the British as punishment. Interestingly, Emery was the grandfather of Richard Henry Dana, author of the classic novel *Two Years before the Mast*.

Dighton firemen stand proudly in uniform in front of their firehouse (the former Andrews Store building), which is decorated for the town's bicentennial celebration in 1912.

Joseph A. Bullard was one of three Dighton soldiers to lose his life in battle. Tragically, he died just one month before the signing of the armistice that would end the First World War.

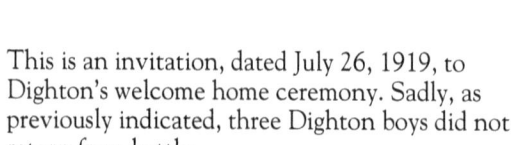

This is an invitation, dated July 26, 1919, to Dighton's welcome home ceremony. Sadly, as previously indicated, three Dighton boys did not return from battle.

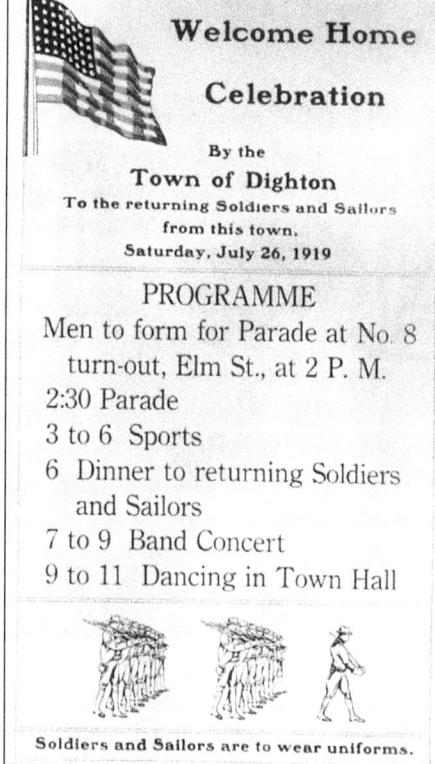

Dighton: Chapter Three
Plow and Pasture

A magnificent pair of draft horses is handled by an unknown Dighton farmer, c. 1915.

This strawberry-packing shed was located on a Dighton farm, c. 1890s. Shortly after 1860, the cultivation of strawberries began to flourish in Dighton and became—at least for a time—the most profitable crop in the area.

By the turn of the century, an influx into Dighton of Portuguese farmers brought the strawberry industry to even greater production than at any time previously (although that is not to say that farmers of other ethnic backgrounds did not also play a vital role). Pictured here is a productive turn-of-the-century Dighton strawberry field.

A Dighton strawberry harvest is shown here c. 1943. By this time, the strawberry industry had begun to wane in Dighton because there were no longer large numbers of family fieldhands available (at this point in the town's history, the children of Portuguese and other farming families often left the small town for more exciting city jobs; additionally, strawberry cultivation did not lend itself to the newer farming technologies). Strawberry cultivation had once been so important to Dighton that, even to the present day, strawberries appear in the town seal.

With present technology, cultivation of the sort pictured in this c. 1910-20 Dighton photograph would indeed be a rare sight today. Still, Dighton, of the three towns addressed in this book, retains its past agrarian flavor to a greater extent than Rehoboth and Swansea.

An unidentified farmer cuts hay in a Dighton field, c. 1920s.

A milk-bottling operation is shown in this c. 1920-30 photograph. Students from the Bristol County Agricultural School engaged in work study here.

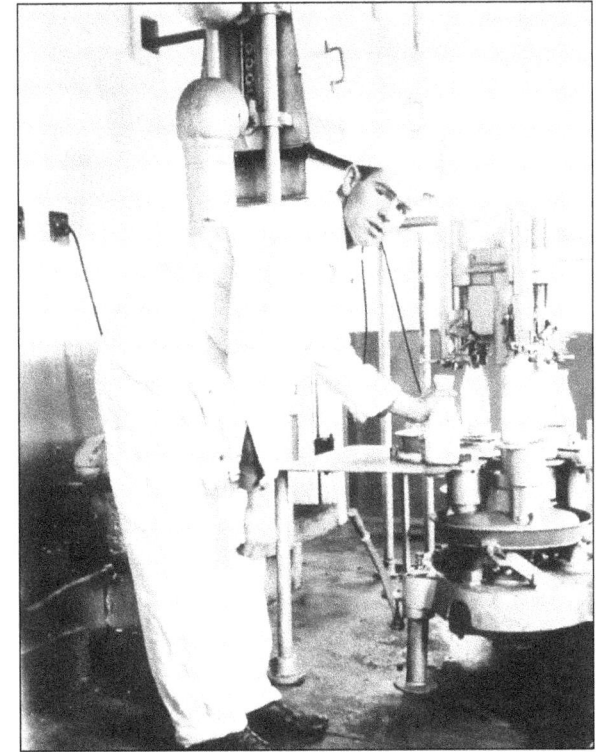

Pictured here, c. 1940s, is a produce display at the Bristol County Agricultural School's early fall fair. The fair still takes place annually.

Prior to the full popular dissemination of electric refrigeration in the 1930s and '40s, ice cutting at ponds in Dighton and elsewhere was an important means of securing ice blocks for storage. Pictured here are farming students at the Bristol County Agricultural School practicing the art.

These milk trucks at a Massachusetts dairy were driven by Dighton students as part of the Bristol County Agricultural School's work study program in the 1920s.

Dighton: Chapter Four
Bibles and Books

The construction of Dighton's Community Church on Elm Street began in 1770 but was held up during the Revolutionary War, when the building was used as sheep pens and as a barracks for soldiers. The church was finally completed in the 1780s. Over the ensuing years, it would vary considerably in the precise nature of its denominations. Its bell was cast by Paul Revere. The old horse block from which riders alighted still stands (see inset).

The First Congregational Church on Center Street in Dighton is pictured here about 1935. Commonly known as the "Brick Church," this building was constructed in 1826 and was the last of three First Congregational churches. The first church stood on Elm Street and burned down in 1767; the second, built on Buck Plain, fell down.

Built with a donation from wealthy benefactors (the Smith family), Smith Memorial Hall, pictured here on a turn-of-the-century postcard, was originally constructed as a parish house for the Dighton Unitarian Church. It is presently used as a recreation hall and classroom building for St. Peter's Roman Catholic Church.

The West Dighton Congregational Church on Goff's Hill in West Dighton is shown here in 1912. Interestingly, the church's old outdoor stone baptismal font still stands, although nowhere near the church. Actually, it is located several miles away across the Rehoboth town line, at the intersection of Reservoir Avenue and Smith Street, which was the site of the original church (built 1779) that preceded the second church building pictured here (built 1796).

This is St. Peter's Roman Catholic Church in 1912. The church was established by Father Smith as a mission church for South Dighton's Portuguese population in 1902 and later evolved into a active parish church. It remains active to this day.

The student body of the Dighton Grammar School posed for this photograph in 1891.

Flat Rock School was located on Williams Street at the end of Main Street. This little school, which accommodated grades one through four, was closed in June of 1928, at which point students in this young age group were transferred to the South School on School Lane.

This was the student body of Dighton's Segreganset School in about 1893. Notice the separate doors for boys and girls. The teacher pictured in the center of the back row is Addie French.

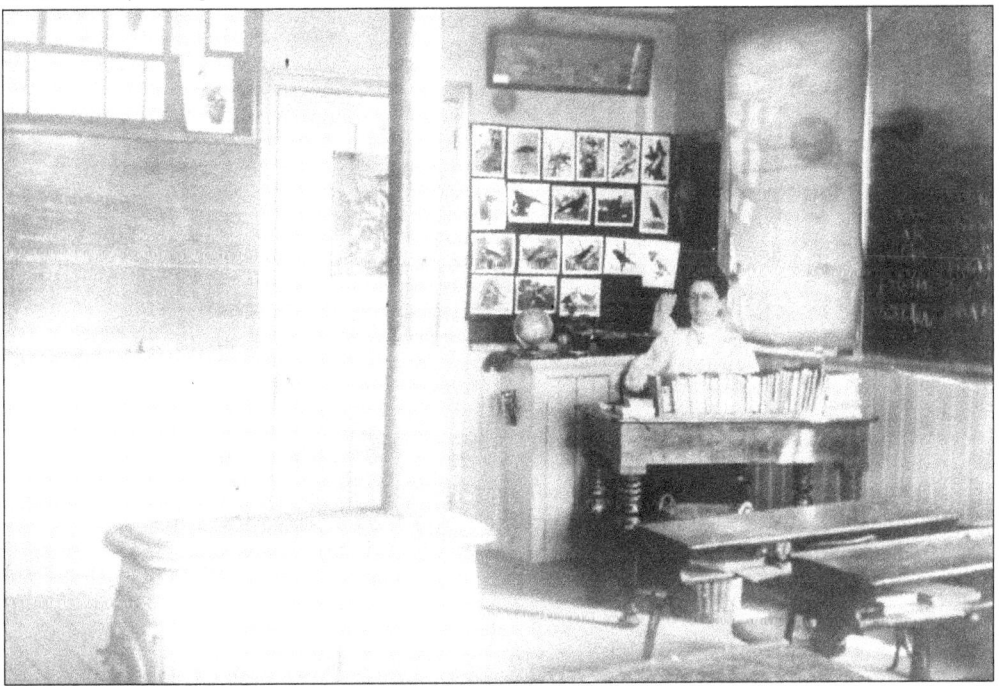

The interior of Dighton's Segreganset School is shown here in 1904. The woman in the photograph is Mabel Emery—one of several different teachers who taught at Segreganset in these early years (another was Addie French).

The fourth grade of South Dighton Grammar School is shown here while on a field trip, c. 1940.

South Dighton's Grammar School is shown here. It was closed in 1951.

The Bristol County Agricultural School in Dighton is shown here shortly after being gutted by a second raging fire in 1936. The school had already suffered a devastating fire in 1923. In both cases, the building was reconstructed.

During the Second World War, as part of the war effort, students at the Dighton schools set up little school banks for selling war bond stamps to classmates.

Dighton students received an award from the government for their wartime efforts in selling government bond stamps. This photograph was taken at some point during the winter of 1942-43.

The Dighton High School, located on Somerset Avenue, is shown here in the 1950s. The building later became a middle school before burning down in 1991.

Dighton: Chapter Five

Mount Hope Memories

In the early part of the century, North Dighton almost stood apart from the rest of the town as its own little "feudal estate" under the absolute control of Joseph K. Milliken, who, in 1901, established the Mount Hope Finishing Company (one of the largest cloth finishing and bleacheries in America). The company is pictured here about 1927, by which time it had become a veritable corporate giant that covered 191.28 acres.

One hundred years earlier, this small bleachery had stood on the North Dighton site where Milliken would eventually build his massive, sprawling Mount Hope Finishing Company. Because of Milliken's prosperous new enterprise, the formerly shabby, run-down surrounding area of North Dighton was transformed into a desirable and prosperous little community which, although still technically part of Dighton, fell under the almost complete control (economically, culturally, and otherwise) of the powerful magnate Milliken.

These women at Milliken's company, c. mid-1920s, are inspecting white cloth. So quality conscious was Milliken that his cloth received forty such inspections before being released for delivery.

A research laboratory, one of several such advanced labs within the Mount Hope Finishing Company's sprawling complex, is pictured here c. 1927. Milliken's progressive use of scientific experimentation and procedure rendered his growing company a state-of-the-art, cutting edge facility with a far-reaching reputation.

Attesting to Milliken's "feudal lordship" (of a benevolent sort) over North Dighton was the fact that many of the houses surrounding the company—some 175 homes—were owned by Milliken and were rented out to his workers at very fair rental prices. This photograph shows how some of the homes appeared—with their well-groomed lawns and attractive shrubbery—in 1927.

The company's average production of 3 million yards of cloth per week required 11 million gallons of water per day. Pictured here is the company reservoir and dam in 1927.

Further extending his control over the North Dighton community surrounding his plant, Milliken transformed an existing mansion (the Nathaniel Wheeler House) into North Dighton's only hospital, pictured here c. 1927. Like other facilities Milliken established in North Dighton, this one was primarily intended for use by his workers, although non-employees were also welcome.

So thoroughly did Milliken and his massive Mount Hope Finishing Company permeate the cultural life of North Dighton that the company newsletter served as a sort of community newspaper, with Milliken himself on the cover of this issue.

This cover indicates that Milliken's *Mount Hope News* was in circulation by at least the early 1920s.

Milliken also established for North Dighton residents a combination fire station, garage, and restaurant. Additionally, he controlled all of North Dighton's municipal services, including electric service (he was instrumental in getting electricity routed to the area from Taunton), water supply, and snow removal. He even established, as shown in this 1927 photograph, a bank, theatre, and clubhouse containing a bowling alley and billiard room. Milliken's North Dighton empire finally ended in 1951, when a disastrous company strike (which split the local populace into opposing factions) forced him to relocate his company to North Carolina. Thereafter, after much struggle and adjustment, North Dighton continued as a general residential community (rather than a company town).

Visit us at
arcadiapublishing.com

www.ingramcontent.com/pod-product-compliance
Lightning Source LLC
Chambersburg PA
CBHW080906100426
42812CB00007B/2175